Defeating the Unbeatable

Defeating the Unbeatable

CRAIG OLSON

RESOURCE *Publications* • Eugene, Oregon

DEFEATING THE UNBEATABLE

Copyright © 2021 Craig Olson. All rights reserved. Except for brief quotations in critical publications or reviews, no part of this book may be reproduced in any manner without prior written permission from the publisher. Write: Permissions, Wipf and Stock Publishers, 199 W. 8th Ave., Suite 3, Eugene, OR 97401.

Scriptures taken from the Holy Bible, New International Version®, NIV®. Copyright © 1973, 1978, 1984, 2011 by Biblica, Inc.™ Used by permission of Zondervan. All rights reserved worldwide. www.zondervan.com The "NIV" and "New International Version" are trademarks registered in the United States Patent and Trademark Office by Biblica, Inc.™

Resource Publications
An Imprint of Wipf and Stock Publishers
199 W. 8th Ave., Suite 3
Eugene, OR 97401

www.wipfandstock.com

PAPERBACK ISBN: 978-1-7252-8916-1
HARDCOVER ISBN: 978-1-7252-8917-8
EBOOK ISBN: 978-1-7252-8918-5

01/19/21

To my amazing wife Tasha. Thank you for pushing me to finish this book and supporting me in the process. Michael and Camdynn, thank you for pushing me to be a better dad *every single day*. I love you all.

Contents

Pregame	1
Spring Training	5
Team	11
Game Time	20
Curveballs	26
Game Fixing	30
Fans	33
Post-Game Celebration	35
Off-Season	38
Love of Game	41
Closer	44
Retirement	48
Grieving in the Victory	53
Confidence	58
Second Career	61

Pregame

*Therefore, with minds that are alert and
fully sober, set your hope on the grace to be
brought to you when Jesus Christ is revealed
at his coming.*

1 PETER 1:13

"YOU HAVE CANCER [OR other serious disease] and it doesn't look good." These words can completely turn a person's or family's world upside down. Lots of people immediately go to the number one source of information . . . the internet. Searching through countless pages of information, you find things like "average life span of six to ten months," "nobody beats this," "no cures available," "clinical trials best option." No matter how long you search, it seems there is nothing but dire news, which puts you into a downward spiral of "why me," "there has to be a mistake," or "I give up." When you go back to the doctor for a follow-up with the next steps, they start sharing numbers and options, and all you want to say is "quit with all the questions and just tell me what to do to make me [or my family member] better!"

However, there is another way to go about this—to be able to grow and enjoy life in spite of a bad prognosis. That answer is Jesus Christ!

Now, I know some of you read that last sentence and got ready to put this book down. Trust me; more than ten years ago I did a very similar thing. I thought, "if Jesus is the answer, then why has God let this happen to my wife, Rachael?" I went through the exact whirlwind I mentioned above and let it engulf me. I didn't lean on anyone for help; I just tried to control everything. I googled and read various online medical pages, which sent me further into a downward spiral. This does not work! All it will do is lead you down a very unhappy and dark road. Sure, you may meet a perfect doctor or find a treatment that does the trick, but without God, it won't be the same. All you will really be doing is just delaying the inevitable. We will all die one day—and then what? If you go down this road of trying to control everything, you will not be on the road that leads to a better life.

The difference is that you will not be *defeating* the "unbeatable"—you will be *withstanding* the "unbeatable." Withstanding the unbeatable means that you might eventually be considered "cancer-free" or "in remission," but eventually you will still pass away . . . to what? What did it take you to get to that point? Did you have any joy leading up to that moment, or were you so doom-and-gloom that you missed it? You may have lived a long life, but where was the good stuff? Defeating the unbeatable means that you acknowledge your situation and want to do what it takes to get healthy, but finding complete healing is not the sole focus of your life. You take the time to enjoy ice cream with your children on a Tuesday. You quietly cuddle with your spouse and watch a football game, or even just listen to good music in the car on the way to an appointment with someone you love. God provides opportunities to focus on the important things. However, this is a process that takes time, and it doesn't mean that you won't have bumps, or sometimes even mountains, that pop up along the way.

Growing up, I was always drawn to baseball. From the time I was little, I remember sitting on the couch or the floor in front of the TV watching TBS or WGN broadcasts of the Braves or Cubs. When I wasn't playing baseball in the backyard with friends and having makeshift home run derbies, I was reading the backs of baseball cards. I was a walking stat book. Throughout my entire childhood to the time I was a junior in college, baseball was a way

PREGAME

of life for me. It provided me with skills and lessons that would help me throughout my life.

In the game of baseball, injuries are a big part of a player's career. One day you are on top of your game and looking forward to a long career and a future big payday, and the next you are on the surgeon's table getting your rotator cuff fixed and wondering if you will ever make it back onto the field. Another big part of baseball is trades; one day you are playing for one team, and the next you are being shipped off to a new team and city. Some players can be traded from a bad team to a good team, but the opposite can happen too; players can go from a good team to a bad team due to their contracts and teammates' performances. As a result, players then endure months of losing and experiencing things that were not in their plans. This is a simple comparison and not as serious as cancer or disease, but provides an illustration some may find relevant.

In the Bible, we meet a man who endured something similar to this. In Genesis chapter 37, we read about Joseph, who was the eleventh of twelve brothers and was known as a dreamer. He dreamed one night that he and his brothers were gathering sheaves of wheat in a field, and then his brothers' sheaves bowed down to his. Later, he dreamed that the sun, moon, and eleven stars bowed down to him. He shared his dreams with his brothers and father, and his brothers got jealous. They didn't like the implication that they might bow down to their younger brother one day. The older brothers decided they'd had enough and decided to sell Joseph to some slave traders. One minute Joseph was on a good team with a family and stability, and the next he was a slave and the lowest of the low. However, through the years of servitude, imprisonment, and betrayal, Joseph decided that he wasn't just going to *withstand* the unbeatable, but *defeat* it. Through God's guidance and love, he eventually worked his way up to be the pharaoh's right-hand man and, during a time of famine, saved the very brothers who had sold him into slavery years before.

After my wife Rachael was first diagnosed with her illness, we were given many other, different diagnoses, making it even more worrisome. First, we found out that her cancer was regrowing only a few months after her first surgery. Then, more than eight years after her initial diagnosis and five years of being off of treatment, we found what we thought was a recurrence. The key to getting through those moments of uncertainty was to put our trust in God. He has a plan for each of our lives, and if we put our trust in Him, He will never leave us and will hold us even in our darkest moments.

Now, this does not mean that if you are diagnosed with an illness and you put your complete trust in God that you will be automatically healed. It *does* mean that you are eternally saved. With this new knowledge, you are better able to roll with the punches that get thrown at you during these times. You can spend more of your energy on enjoying the moments around you. It is amazing how much we miss when our focus is on dying rather than on living. For example, in our story, my wife was diagnosed with a grade IV glioblastoma, which is the most deadly kind of brain tumor and has an average life expectancy of twelve to eighteen months. When the doctors came into her hospital room and told us the news, we were absolutely devastated and didn't know what to think. However, in that moment, Rachael gathered herself and with complete confidence and strength stated, "Let's get started." In moments like these, when it seems like your world has just been thrown completely upside down, God can still shine His light into the darkness and chaos..

In baseball, there are warm-ups before each game. During this time, players stretch, take batting practice, field ground balls, and play catch. Basically, this is their time for final preparations for the opponent they are about to face. Once you know the opponent you are facing, whether it's cancer or another trial, this warm-up period is the time to choose whether you are going to step up to the plate.

Where do you stand in your beliefs? Are you in the warm-up stage of life, ready for difficulties to be thrown at you, or are you just going about life with no real purpose?

Spring Training

> *Be always on the watch, and pray that you may be able to escape all that is about to happen, and that you may be able to stand before the Son of Man.*
>
> LUKE 21:36

EACH FEBRUARY, JUST FOUR short months after the final pitch of the previous World Series, excitement begins to fill the air in Florida and Arizona. Baseball players start arriving to prepare for the long, 162-game season that will start in April and, hopefully, end after the playoffs in October. Spring training begins with pitchers and catchers showing up first, followed by the rest of the players. It's an opportunity for veterans (players who have been around for a while) to continue rehabbing injuries, trying new pitches, or stretching out one more good season. It is also an opportunity for rookies (first-year players) to try and break through to the major league.

During spring training, coaches take players through fundamental drills to help their bodies remember the movements. The intensity and frequency of these drills are much more substantial in spring training than they are in the regular season, when there aren't as many days off to practice. Another difference between spring training and the regular season is that the number of players on a team at any given time is significantly higher during spring training. This is largely due to the fact that teams want to evaluate as many of their players as possible and prevent overworking their veteran players before regulation play starts.

You will have battles with the unbeatable that are similar to spring training. With an initial diagnosis, or even prior to the diagnosis, you may face a revolving door of doctors, nurses, and specialists trying to figure out what is going on. Then comes the decision-making process. For instance, maybe you will need to decide between several different hospitals or possibly different departments within a hospital. Maybe you have people in your life saying that they will be there no matter what with the best of intentions, but will cut themselves out as your struggles become more challenging (and honestly, life happens to them too). You may have to make tough decisions in which you do some of the cutting. While this may seem cold, unfortunately, it will happen. It may be due to logistics as you travel or even move for treatments or it may have to do with a person's attitude.

For Rachael and me, this started on the very first day of her battle. When the ambulance showed up, the paramedics asked me which hospital to take her to. This was an extremely difficult situation for me to even consider, given that my loved one was in need of immediate help and the paramedics were supposed to be the experts. The answer to this seemingly basic question was like trying to decide whether I wanted the Babe Ruth or the Hank Aaron. However, the impact of my answer began a ripple effect of the different choices we were going to have to make regarding who would continue this battle with us and who would take on a lesser role. The days that followed were full of all kinds of doctors and nurses trying to figure out what was going on with Rachael. As things became clearer and clearer, we were able to begin the cutting process. The decision of which hospital to go to led to meeting a specific doctor who had access to valuable information that led us to Seattle, Washington, instead of Rochester, Minnesota. With these decisions, the number of people close to us on our spring training team began to dwindle. Many of the people we cut lived in Fargo, North Dakota, which made it easier for us to make the cuts. It was difficult leaving them, but it was necessary for our journey.

Spring Training

In the book of Judges, we can find a perfect example of how God took his people through a "spring training" in their own lives before heading into battle. Specifically, in Judges 7, we see how God helped a soon-to-be leader named Gideon make important decisions about those he would take into battle with him. Gideon's army started with 32,000 men, which was already way fewer men than the Midianites they were going to face in battle. By the time Gideon actually went into battle, God had commanded him to cut his army down to 300 soldiers. God knew the specific people Gideon needed in his army to be successful and bring Him glory. In the same way, He knows the specific people we need in our lives as we face difficult times.

While spring training can be an exciting and fun time for fans and for players looking to make a splash, it is also a very stressful time. Coaches and managers have to decide whether they have the right players on their team—and which players they need to get rid of. Similarly, this time in your battle will also be very stressful. You will have many decisions thrown at you which you are not prepared for. You will have to decide treatment choices, location to pursue treatment, and, if you have children, how you are going to do this while caring for them. All of this will happen while you're also dealing with the heartbreak of knowing that the struggles are just starting. Be willing to step out of your shell and ask people for help. Baseball teams don't have one single person making all of the decisions. The manager, who is the head of the baseball team, uses his coaches to help him make decisions. He has in-depth conversations with them and then uses that information to make better decisions. In the same way, lean on those around you to help you make important decisions.

When Rachael was initially diagnosed with her illness in 2009, we had been married just over a year and were going to college nowhere near our families. We went through all of our initial struggles trying to balance everything by ourselves. The biggest issue we had to face was that we did not have health insurance, which was a major obstacle to finding a surgeon willing to do brain surgery without knowing how they would be paid. We did not have children at the time, which was one thing we didn't have to make decisions about.

We talked for several years after her diagnosis of how fortunate we felt that we didn't have any children during that time because we had no clue what we would have done. We continued through the battle of her initial fight with brain cancer, and she did exceptionally well and was able to go off treatment in 2011. She was not cancer-free, but the doctors said that she was stable, which was a blessing.

After surviving that season, we embarked on a new spring training in 2016. This new season was the result of being told that Rachael's brain cancer had returned and, based on the growth of the tumor, we needed to make decisions in a hurry. We went through all of the same struggles as before, but in addition, this time we had two handsome miracle boys. The ages of the boys did not help either, as Michael was three years old and Camdynn was one year old. The struggle of going through this battle all over again while meeting the needs of our boys was extremely difficult and created an even greater sense of urgency. Leaning on our prior experience, we pushed through the spring training for this new battle at a much quicker pace. One verse that helped me through this time in spite of everything was Isaiah 41:10: "So do not fear, for I am with you; do not be dismayed, for I am your God. I will strengthen you and help you; I will uphold you with my righteous right hand." No matter how bad it may seem, how challenging a situation is, or how lonely you may feel, remember that God is always there.

I know that, on a personal level, I have grown year after year in my "spring trainings." I have gone from being the rookie who is there to impress everyone at all costs to the young star enjoying the great times to the veteran just trying to get a little more out of his career. In the beginning, I put up walls and made sure I was the rock for everyone else. At this point, I really lost my understanding of who I was. During that "rookie" time, being the "stable one" was my defense mechanism. Each one of us has our own defense mechanisms, and denying myself for everyone else's sake is mine. However, down the line, it began to wear me very thin. I was putting my trust in myself to do everything instead of giving everything to God and leaning on Him to guide me in the struggles. If I had given it all to Him and sought Him during this time, things would have been much different. I am not saying that Rachael's cancer would have just disappeared, but the emotional drain I felt that prevented me from supporting Rachael and our boys would have been less of a problem.

As we moved into our "star" spring trainings, things were going so well that we weren't too worried about anything. Rachael was doing great and we were having the time of our married lives. People were calling Rachael their poster child for brain cancer. The problem with these types of spring trainings is that they can go to your head. I became blind to certain things and went back to my habit of putting God on the back burner. Psalm 103:2 states, "Praise the Lord, my soul, and forget not all his benefits." I was basically doing the opposite of this verse. I started to forget all He had done and focused on everything being good. There is a benefit to focusing on the good, for sure, but it was more of a "look what we have done" versus "look what God has done."

Then the next thing you know, you are a "veteran" trying to squeak out one more year, sitting at spring training reflecting on your career and hoping this isn't it, and wondering how you have gone from the young "rookie" with all the defense mechanisms to not knowing how to change. This is a struggle I dealt with around the time of Rachael's rediagnosis. I had built up tall walls and didn't know how to let them down and be vulnerable to myself and others. Emotional walls can come down a couple of different ways. They can come down quickly and become a massive mess, but provide an opportunity for earlier rebuilding, or they can come down slowly. In this case, little by little, the wall is broken down, but it takes a lot of time. As a result, the struggle can last much longer with no real help in sight. The latter is the type of breakdown I had. This resulted in me missing out on things due to trying to act strong.

With these ups and downs, just like with spring training, our team changed over the years, ebbing and flowing from larger numbers to smaller numbers. Each spring training season provided something unique, whether it was short term or long term. Finally, in my "veteran" years of this journey, I have been able to identify my struggles with walls and let people into my life who have helped me examine myself. For me, those people were men from my church who stepped out to meet me where I was. They saw that I was in need, and God helped prepare my heart to be open to talking to and leaning on these men. I now consider them some of my closest and best friends. For you, the people you lean on to help break down your walls may come from other places, but just be willing to allow them to help.

Where are you in your current journey? Are you going to spring training as a rookie, a young star, or a veteran? Be honest with yourself; it could make all the difference in how enjoyable this season is for you.

Team

Two are better than one, because they have a good return for their labor: If either of them falls down, one can help the other up.

ECCLESIASTES 4:9–10

IN BASEBALL, THERE ARE about twenty-five players on an active roster during the regular season, which means they are dressed out for each game and ready to play. This number can dip, though, depending on minor injuries and if pitchers need a rest. In addition to these active players, there are several coaches and a manager. Each person has a specific and important role to play to help their team achieve success. They are all headed by the manager, who is in charge of making decisions and guiding the rest of the team. In order to defeat the unbeatable, you will need to have a team yourself. For each person, this will look different. Maybe you have a very tight-knit family who will be right there with you the whole way. Or you might have a core group of close friends who will stick with you no matter what.

Good teammates include people who are willing to drop everything and help you out any way they can, no matter what time it is. Just like in baseball, you want people on your team who can provide different kinds of support. For instance, Rachael and I lived near her mom, and she was what you would call our utility player. She was able to wear multiple hats and help out in many different ways. This included coming over in the middle of the night to watch our boys as I took Rachael to the emergency room, going with us on trips to the hospitals to help me, or even just spending time with Rachael and the boys when I need a break.

Our church family was willing to take care of our boys if needed and provide emotional support. The school where I taught also helped with the boys and provided us with dinners, allowing me to focus on spending time with our family. Even though my parents lived seven hours away from us, they were also part of our team, as they provided emotional support whenever we needed it, as well as a source of escape for us to get away and travel.

There are people that God has put into many different parts of our lives for specific reasons. Sometimes we don't even realize it until after the fact. For instance, just before Rachael had her recurrence, I took a job at a school that was five minutes from our house instead of thirty minutes. I figured it was meant to be and it would be easy to get home sooner. However, the staff I work with went above and beyond—they all pitched in, provided support, and made me feel like we were all in it together and that they were a part of our family. I had a small group of people like this in my prior school, but the size of my support group grew from four people to twenty people. This was not how I envisioned it, but God knew.

Accepting these teammates has not always been easy, though. When it comes to cancer or any other significant illness or death, most people become nervous. They don't know how to act, they become awkward, and many eventually just can't handle it. Frankly, this is okay; those are not the people you need to focus on. Your team should be made up of people who put their cleats on each day and toe the rubber with you no matter what. There were several people in our journey who joined up with us and walked alongside us for a bit and quickly realized, "nah, I can't do this." Please note that this does not make them bad people. It doesn't mean that they can't still be a part of your journey; they just aren't your best source of help.

The coaches are the next level of a team. They are the ones who have knowledge in specific areas. In baseball, the team has a pitching coach, a hitting coach, a fielding coach, and other focused coaches. They only focus on their specific area of expertise with their players. When battling the unbeatable, you will want to have the best coaches you can. Typically, your coaches will be your doctors. Unless you are a doctor, you will not have that same level of expertise in the area of your concern, so you are going to want to make sure you trust your doctors. That does not mean that you don't continue to ask questions and do more research, but it does mean that they are rich with knowledge. They are living and working within this specific area of concern on a daily basis and know what problems can arise.

For Rachael, her coaches were her neurology team. She had her neuro-oncologist, who focused on her chemo treatments and explained her MRI results to us. She had her radiation oncologist, who was in charge of all radiation therapies. She had a radiologist, who interpreted her MRIs. In addition, she had countless nurses who shared their expertise. Each one of these people provideed unique care and worked together to provide us with the best options moving forward.

Generally speaking, there is a major difference between a pitcher who "has a cup of coffee" in the majors and a Hall of Fame pitcher. The Hall of Famer may start out with less overall talent than the "cup of coffee" pitcher, but they are students of the game. They are always taking in new information and asking questions, and they're not afraid to second-guess something. On the other hand, the "cup of coffee" pitcher relies on their talent alone and does not continue to learn. This results in yet another pitcher in a long list of major league talent who never reached full potential. In terms of your battle, arming yourself with knowledge of the illness that is affecting you or your loved one will go a long way in your ability to put coaches in your game that you trust.

Another thing to remember is that while doctors can provide you with ideas and direction, it is up to you to follow their lead. Your decisions still come down to you and your attitude during this battle. You will come across doctors with a wealth of knowledge, but no people skills. They will tell it like it is with very little emotion. We had those moments a few times in our journey. While these doctors were great coaches in terms of providing expertise, they were negative about the expected outcomes. This is a key choice—whether you are going to give up or beat the unbeatable.

Rachael and I wavered at times with this choice, typically right after those kinds of meetings. You go in expecting things to be okay and come out feeling like you've just had your death sentence written. God is the one who has the final say, so let Him decide how things will turn out. It is all right to be down for a while, but make a decision to still enjoy life and the moments you are given. Early on in Rachael's battle, we had times of being severely distraught and not feeling like speaking for most of our three-hour trip home. However, over time, we began to change because of God's grace. We began talking more about our feelings in the moment and were completely honest with each other. As we opened up, things began to change in me and in Rachael. While we were still frustrated and exhausted, we were also thankful. We were thankful that God had put Rachael in a location where we had doctors who were honest, but in general showed compassion. We were thankful that Rachael was still alive, and that in spite of only being given fifteenish months to live, she made it more than eight years. But this was not because of us; it was all because of God.

One thing to understand with all these coaches is that, yes, they do have immense knowledge in their fields, but they will have many other patients they are working with. As a result, the time it takes to get back to you with specific information may be longer than you would like. That is why you need to be knowledgeable in the area of your concern and be willing to push for guidance. You will also need to put in some time doing research on your own and discussing the information you find with your coaches. For me, this broadened my knowledge of the human brain more than I could ever imagine, and this knowledge became increasingly beneficial as we went further down our path. With Rachael's recurrence and related seizures, we found ourselves going to the ER on multiple occasions. We lived in a relatively small town where most of the doctors had little to no knowledge of brain tumors and the current forms of treatment. As a result, most of the time I had to guide the doctors through what worked, what didn't, and what types of treatments she was on, and because I did my own research, I was able to use correct terms and speak with confidence. This helped make our ER trips much more effective and allowed for quicker resolutions of her seizures. Remember, even with the best coaches, there will be times when you need to take control and have the necessary knowledge to make proactive decisions.

All of the positions mentioned in this chapter allow you to choose who will be on your team. However, there is one position that cannot be filled by anyone on this earth, and that is the manager. In order to defeat the unbeatable, the manager position must be filled by God. This is not negotiable. You can't read your demands to God and expect Him to agree. It is the other way around. He has expectations of us. However, these are very easy to find and are laid out well for us in a manual. That manual is the Bible, and in it, we find the answers to how we are supposed to meet God's expectations.

Some might say that the Bible is just a bunch of stories written for people who need a "crutch" to make it through life. However, who are the people who need "crutches?" The ones who are broken and need something or someone to help them become healthy. But the thing to remember is that these stories are not made up like the stories we find in children's books that we read at bedtime. The stories we find in the Bible are true accounts of godly people who went through hard times and needed support to make it through.

To be honest, early on in Rachael's journey through cancer, I had some questions about the stories in the Bible. My questions were not about whether those things had actually happened, but about whether those miraculous things could happen for Rachael. I didn't believe or understand just how big God actually is, so I had some massive struggles as I tried to negotiate with God. I basically wanted Him to take care of some areas and let me handle the rest. All this did was cause bigger problems for me and for the people around me.

When I finally decided to let God be the manager and have complete control, things began to change. Rachael and I enjoyed more things in our lives despite the struggles. We began to live for God as He took more control. As a result, we saw blessings we could have only dreamed of. My only regret is that I wish I had come to this realization a lot earlier.

Defeating the Unbeatable

Think about the people Jesus healed in the Bible. The cripple by the fountain waited every day for someone to help him for years on end, and Jesus walked right up to him and told him to get up and walk (John 5:1–8). This man needed a "crutch" to marginally improve his quality of life. However, Jesus took it a step further and not only helped the man but completely healed him. Similarly, with the blind man in Mark 8:22–26, Jesus didn't just help him but once again completely healed him. In moments when people felt completely helpless, Jesus met them where they were and helped them.

One thing to note about the people Jesus healed is that they showed faith that the seemingly impossible could actually happen. Jesus asked the cripple by the fountain if he wanted to get well in John 5. The man showed his faith when Jesus told him to get up and walk and the man didn't say anything—he just did as he was told.

At the beginning of our journey, my faith was far from that type of faith. In fact, my faith prevented me from thinking in any way, shape, or form about what would happen down the road because I wanted to live in the present. My thinking was, "Rachael's tumor is too big. It is in a bad spot. Why are we wasting time here?" The longer we progressed in our journey and saw the blessings bestowed on us, I realized that the impossible could happen.

My understanding of the impossible evolved over time as well. *Impossible* is a term we use to define things that humans can't possibly do. However, in God's vocabulary, everything is possible because He can do anything. Rachael and I put our faith in God that we would have children someday even if they weren't biologically ours, so we declined to freeze Rachael's eggs. Now we have two amazing miracle biological boys that were only possible with God. I still struggle with the breadth of God's power and what He can do, so constant reminders of His abilities are important.

If we are honest with ourselves, we are all broken in many ways. Every day we do things we are not proud of (and that God isn't proud of, either). However, through Jesus' death and resurrection and the promises fulfilled through Him, we are saved and know that we have an eternal "crutch" that is always with us whenever we need the support. However, He is also with us in the good, so don't forget that!

Team

The Bible is very focused on the importance of having support systems. You don't need to look any further than Jesus Himself. During his three years of ministry, He had a core group of people He kept close to Him: His disciples. These were men with whom He lived and fellowshipped on a daily basis. He let them know about the struggles in His life and allowed them to live through everything, good and bad, with Him. He did all of this in spite of the fact that He is God and all-knowing, and He could have done everything on His own.

There are many more examples of support systems in the Bible, including Moses, who was helped many times by his brother Aaron (Exod 4:27–31; 17:10–12). Daniel had Shadrach, Meshach, and Abednego, who were willing to be thrown into King Nebuchadnezzar's fiery furnace rather than bow to a false god (Dan 3:14–18). Even David, who killed the giant Goliath and eventually became Israel's king, had a very close core group of friends that included Jonathan, who he trusted for wisdom and support. Don't try to defeat the unbeatable alone!

Allowing others to help you can look like Moses allowing his brother Aaron and his friend Hur to hold his arms up as the Israelites battle the Amalekites (Exod 17:10–12). While Moses held his arms up, the Israelites had the upper hand in the battle; however, when Moses put his arms down, the Amalekites started winning. Without the support of Aaron and Hur, Moses could not keep his arms lifted to protect the Israelites. For me, in the beginning of our journey, I never let people help "hold my arms up." In fact, I kept going and going without slowing down and eventually burned myself out. Unfortunately, several problems arose because of this. First, I became physically exhausted and unhealthy. Second, I drifted in my relationship with God. This caused me to drift from Rachael too.

As the years progressed and I had a few "aha" moments about myself, I slowly began leaning on others for support. Now, I still do struggle with this, as I am overly proud when it comes to providing for my family. I know this is a struggle, so I pray for God's help all the time. He knows where we struggle, but He still wants us to share our struggles with Him and ask Him for help.

Defeating the Unbeatable

The problem is that many people act like free agents who sign short-term contracts. They sign up to have God be their manager when things are difficult, but when things are going well, they find someone or something else to be the manager of their lives. When this happens, inevitably a curveball comes their way and they scramble to figure out how to make it through. There will be times of uncertainty throughout life, but as long as you have accepted Jesus as your Lord and Savior, you are never alone!

Another important position to consider is the team captain. This is the player voted on by the rest of the team. Team captains are the player that the team feels they want to look up to for guidance and wisdom. The captain is often the face of an entire team. For instance, when most baseball fans hear the name Derek Jeter, one of the things that comes to mind is "The Captain" for the New York Yankees. However, just like other positions, captains still lean on others for support.

We have the perfect example of a team captain for us all: Jesus Christ. To this day, He is the face of the kingdom of God. In the Bible, Jesus provides us with a clear picture of how we should live in the face of trials. Throughout His entire life, Jesus struggled with opposition from all sides. One example of this comes after He was baptized and went off into the wilderness to be tempted by Satan (Matt 4:1–11). The way Jesus responded to Satan's temptations shows us how we should respond in the face of obstacles. Jesus knew that He should not test God, but rather trust in Him. In the same way, we are to trust God. This does not mean everything will become easier, but we will find hope.

Near the end of His life, Jesus again faced major adversity as He was handed over to be crucified. This is where we see a perfect picture as to what it means to defeat the unbeatable. Since the beginning of time, God had a plan to have Jesus die for our sins (Gen 3:15). As Jesus faced the reality of being crucified, He asked God to take the struggle away from Him. However, after His request, His next sentence was "yet not my will, but yours be done" (Luke 22:42). Jesus had the ability to save His life, but instead He put His trust in the manager.

Team

As baseball teams go through the season, there are times when teams feel they need to shake things up or make a change at certain positions. This is typically done in the form of a trade, which means that they bring a new player in from another team to replace one of their own players. In the same way, if someone on your team is not meeting your expectations, you can "trade" them. For instance, if there is a doctor who you feel is not meeting your needs, find a new one. Rachael and I did this a couple of times. One of the "trades" we made was because we did not feel that the doctor was compassionate enough. Now, I know that compassion is not the main focus of a doctor's job, but if you don't feel like your doctor is making you feel like they care about you, then it is your prerogative to make a change.

In addition to making your own changes, there will be times when God or one of the coaches may make a trade. This could be due to doctors not feeling like they have the expertise to meet your needs or making a career choice that takes them away from you. Rachael had this happen during her treatments when a doctor moved to a new hospital and required us to choose a new doctor. However, in spite of all these changes, whether you make them or someone else does, one constant will be that God is always managing your team.

Take a moment and think about who your team consists of. Can you put people into different positions? Do you know who all your coaches are? Is God honestly your manager or just another coach?

Game Time

Be alert and of sober mind. Your enemy the devil prowls around like a roaring lion looking for someone to devour. Resist him, standing firm in the faith.

1 PETER 5:8–9

WITH THE TEAM IN place and the preparation work all done, it is time to perform. In baseball, a typical game consists of nine innings, in which teams take turns trying to score runs before the other team gets them out three times. Games are full of highs and lows for players, coaches, and fans. However, if you have prepared well as a team, you can be very successful.

All of this holds true when facing the unbeatable. If you have a great group of teammates, you can succeed. However, in order to enjoy the game and win, you must have God as your manager. If He is the leader of your team, you'll know you can trust in Him during the adversities that will take place. That doesn't mean you will walk all over your enemy and beat it easily, but it *does* mean that you can take comfort in difficult times.

In a major league baseball season, each team plays 162 games. The record for most wins in a season is 116 by the 2001 Seattle Mariners. With that being said, the most successful regular-season team in history still lost forty-six times *and* didn't win the World

Series. In the same way, I can guarantee that you will have losses in your battle with cancer or illness.

In the Bible, there are many stories of God-fearing people who trusted Him but still had struggles. For instance, Job was a very faithful man. God even went so far as to praise how much Job loved and followed Him in front of Satan (Job 1:8). Satan, in turn, wanted to put Job's faith to the test. As the first chapter of Job continues, we read that Job ended up losing his livestock, servants, and children in one evening. Yes, Job became depressed and tore his clothes, but he did not once turn from God. Instead, Job did the opposite; he worshipped and honored God. Throughout the entire book of Job, we read about extremely difficult situations that would push any other man to his breaking point. Job's wife told him to curse God (Job 2:9) and a couple of his friends suggested similar things, but not once did Job dishonor God.

In the beginning of our journey, I thought that if God was truly with us, Rachael would be healed quickly. When she wasn't, I lost trust in God. I was going through a difficult stretch, a losing streak. It seemed like every new obstacle that was thrown at us made us fall further and further behind. However, Rachael continued to push through, and seeing her faith pushed me to work on mine. Slowly, we started to get some wins. Rachael had stable MRIs. Then she had other slight improvements. Doctors' outlooks seemed more and more positive, and it seemed like there was some hope after all.

All of a sudden, we were getting more wins and feeling closer than ever to God. Of course, this trap of praising God when things are going well is easy to fall into. I fell into this trap along the road. We know of Job and the struggles he faced, yet he still loved God even in the worst of times. Conversely, we seem to pay attention to praising God only when good things are happening until, finally, something bad happens and we find ourselves on the other end of the spectrum. For us, that day came when Rachael had a seizure and it threw me for a loop. Luckily, I realized that Satan was trying to use this slip as an opportunity to gain ground.

We're not the only ones who go through trials and losing streaks like these. Even Jesus's disciples went through trials and failures when they were with Jesus. They were tested in their faith and failed several times as they were learning. One example is found in Mark 4:40, when Jesus calmed a storm at sea that terrified his disciples, and He said to them, "Why are you so afraid? Do you still have no faith?" At this moment, the apostles lost, as they didn't have complete faith. However, Jesus did not just give up on them. He continued teaching them, and they eventually became key contributors to the Bible and Christianity.

For us, having God as our manager allowed me to devote my time and energy to being available for Rachael whenever she needed me. We trusted Him with my job, and He put me in a position as a school teacher where I was able to make myself available for Rachael by having time off to run her to appointments and help in other ways. He helped us get a home close to Rachael's mom, which allowed her to help me with the boys.

Making God our manager also allowed me, as the caregiver, to take time for myself. Through Him, we made relationships with people who watched over and helped Rachael when I needed "time off." This is important, because if I had not been given those opportunities, I would have been no help to Rachael because I would have been burned out. This is important for anyone who is a caregiver. Know that it is all right to ask people for help so you can take care of yourself. It will be hard to leave your loved one, but if you are exhausted and unable to help them to the best of your ability, you won't be able to meet their needs when you need to. Prior to your loved one getting sick, I am sure you had a hobby or two that you enjoyed doing. Don't stop them! These can help keep you sane!

I know many people struggle with the idea of leaving their loved one so they can take breaks. You feel selfish and like your loved one needs you. However, you aren't selfish, and don't worry—that is what cell phones are for. In the beginning of our journey, I only left Rachael alone for about an hour at most so I could grab a bite to eat and use the bathroom. I would then jump right back into another long stretch of being at her disposal. I know now that Rachael didn't always appreciate that I became overly watchful of her. This frustrated her and even strained our relationship a bit.

Sure, there were times when she definitely wanted me to be with her, but as we progressed further into our journey, this changed, and after realizing the consequences of my continued hovering, I allowed myself time away.

The benefits of this time were immediately recognizable. Rachael seemed more rested when she saw me, and I was more relaxed after my time away and better able to meet her needs. Even the best baseball players need time off to recuperate for the next stretch. In fact, Jesus consistently found opportunities to pull away from others to quiet places where he could rest, reset, and be with his heavenly Father.

When a pitcher is no longer effective, the manager has to decide what to do. Does he keep the tired pitcher in the game or does he chose one of his relief pitchers? If he chooses a relief pitcher, he still has to decide among the seven, who all bring something different to the field. Some pitchers are only good for a couple of different types of batters while others are good for any hitter. Some are so specialized they only face one or two batters. However, the manager has to plan by looking at the upcoming batters, how many innings are left in the game, and how often the pitchers have been used. Their choice is important to the team's success.

Growing up, I was a starting pitcher, and I averaged about six innings each time I started. Since this was taxing on my arm, I would typically have around four days off before I would pitch again. This meant other teammates would have to pitch for our team. In the same way, allowing others to help take some of the weight off your shoulders will be key. That way you are rested and ready to be the best you can be for the big moments.

God brings people into our lives to help us through different situations for different purposes. During the school year, the staff at my school provided for us in many tangible ways. Then, once the school year ended, He brought in new relief. Without prompting from us of any kind, our church family began blessing us with help during the summer.

This is not to say that you won't have struggles during a game. Just like in a baseball game, you are going to have bad at-bats, you are going to make errors, and you will have innings where you're losing. We are all susceptible to trials that may feel like they can't possibly get any worse, but they can and will get better if you are being managed by God. This doesn't necessarily mean that you will be cured, but it does mean that you will be able to enjoy the simple things in life and defeat the unbeatable.

Another component of baseball games that can be just plain annoying are the hecklers who come to games just to yell at and get under the skin of players. These are typically fans who have done research on your team and know rumors and facts that they feel will distract the players from what is happening on the field. In the same way, you will run into hecklers who will try to do the same thing to you. They will say things like "I had a friend who only made it a couple of months" or "if God really exists, why hasn't He healed you?" The second phrase in particular has a way of planting a very tiny seed of doubt that, if not acknowledged and squashed, will slowly grow. Not only can these people get under your skin and make you feel lost and scared but they can also make you angry. This can cause you to lash out at others when they haven't done anything wrong. These feelings are totally normal and expected, but you still need to be aware of the possible consequences.

We heard similar things throughout Rachael's fight. I admit I allowed several of those tiny seeds to take root in me at different times. When Rachael was initially diagnosed, I asked God, "why would you let this happen to Rachael? What has she ever done to deserve this?" God can take this type of question. He is the God of everything and therefore big enough to handle it. If God can't handle us asking tough questions, then it would be hard for us to believe in Him. However, I say a tiny seed of doubt was planted in this question because I was essentially implying that God had caused this to happen to Rachael. I lacked understanding of the true power of God's love. As we have continued down this journey, I have learned that His love and plan are so much bigger than we can possibly imagine.

I would have never believed that Rachael's story could reach throughout the United States through different avenues, as well as to other countries. God has used Rachael and her "game time" approach to help others going through cancer and other struggles in their own lives. God is with you through everything. Believe that truth and allow Him to hold you!

Are you ready for game time? What approach are you taking to becoming successful?

Curveballs

Consider it pure joy, my brothers and sisters, whenever you face trials of many kinds, because you know that the testing of your faith produces perseverance. Let perseverance finish its work so that you may be mature and complete, not lacking anything.

JAMES 1:2-4

GROWING UP, I SPENT most of my summers playing baseball as a pitcher, and my best pitch was my curveball. This pitch gets its name from its curved path on the way to home plate. This change of direction is orchestrated by the pitcher, and the goal is to catch the batter off guard. When facing the unbeatable, you will be thrown many curveballs. If the devil was a major league pitcher, he would be a guaranteed first-ballot Hall of Famer just because of his curveballs. Just when you feel like life is beginning to fall into place and things are looking up, here comes that big nasty curveball that looks just like every other pitch.

These curveballs may happen one at a time or in bunches. For us, they seemed to happen in bunches. For instance, in October 2016, Rachael had a routine MRI. She had been doing very well up to that point and things were looking great. In fact, this was her first MRI since her doctor had switched her from every four months to every six months because she was doing so well. As we prepared for that MRI, we were expecting a fastball right over the plate—that we would go in, get good news, and head home. However, we swung and missed in a big way. Rachael's MRI ended up showing changes that needed to be monitored. We left the doctor's office in complete shock, like someone frozen by a 12:6 curveball. This devastating pitch looks like it is going to be a high pitch, then seems to have the bottom drop out of it, which would look like going from 12:00 to 6:00 on a clock face. We discovered that Rachael had to have two more MRIs over the next two months, and if she didn't get on some form of treatment, the results would probably become catastrophic in less than a year. It was like we were facing a pitcher who threw three curveballs and struck us out. We had just started dusting ourselves off from the latest curveball when we were dealt another one.

Around 1:00 one morning soon after that, I woke up to our bed shaking. I initially thought it was Rachael's cat and started to yell at him, but I quickly realized Rachael was having a seizure. She ended up having three more over the course of several hours. Once again, we were back in the ambulance and emergency room. These seizures happened right after Rachael had finished six cycles of chemo to try and reverse the growths found on her MRI. The doctors at the local hospital did a CT scan that didn't show anything concerning, but her blood counts did show that her magnesium was low. The doctors presumed that this was the cause of her seizures. This seemed like a small curveball we could adjust to and keep swinging.

However, when fighting a disease that is often multi-layered, don't put your guard down when you seem to adjust to the curveball; be prepared to swing at another one. In our case, Rachael ended up back in the ER ten days later with an identical situation. This led to more questions that could only be answered with an MRI. She finally got an MRI, and this is where we found out just how big a curveball this was. The scan showed a new spot that was the culprit of the seizures.

Showing just how much this evil disease works, this was not our last curveball. We had a plan of attack on how we were going to deal with the new spot, but there was a problem. Once again, another curveball was thrown our way as the doctors explained that the radiologist found an additional spot that could only be treated with chemo.

After you face several curveballs in a row, there is another opponent who becomes stronger. The devil senses your vulnerability during a situation like this and tries to work his way in. He does this by finding your weak spots and attacking them. That's why it is important to lean on your manager, God, for guidance and leadership. It is only through His lead that you will be able to truly defeat the unbeatable and the other opponent, who is always waiting to throw his own pitches at you. I was not in tune with my own weak spots, and the devil was ready and began attacking.

The key to hitting a curveball is to keep your weight back and identify the spin. When a pitcher throws a curveball, the baseball will create a circle as it's spinning toward the plate, and if the hitter identifies that spin early, he can adjust to the pitch. In the same way, it is important when fighting a deadly disease to identify its "spin." Not all curveballs can be identified until they happen, but if you can "foul them off," or adjust to them to keep moving forward, then you can better prepare for the next ones.

Rachael's MRIs and seizures were curveballs we did not identify early. In fact, they were not even on our radar, since she had been doing very well for over five years. However, by leaning on God as our manager, Rachael was still able to have a positive attitude and enjoy the opportunities she had in spite of her struggles.

In Mark 10, Jesus provides a great example to help us understand that entering the kingdom of God is not something that should be easy. He talked to a rich young ruler who came to Him and asked, "what must I do to inherit eternal life?" (Mark 10:17). Jesus asked the ruler a series of questions and finished by explaining that the man lacked one thing. He told the man to sell all of his valuables and come and follow Him. At this, the young man became discouraged and left. Jesus explained that "it is easier for a camel to go through the eye of a needle than for someone who is rich to enter the kingdom of God" (Mark 10:25). This example has given me comfort through the curveballs we have faced. It helps me understand that regardless of what we do in life, if we want to be eternally with Jesus, we will have struggles. These struggles will come from evil, and how we face them will determine where we end up. That is why I continue to use the phrase "defeating the unbeatable." In the end, we will all die and leave this world. However, if you believe in God, you will have a brand new life. Jesus has paid for our sins, and therefore we can enter the eternal life that God has planned for us. Death cannot defeat us, but in Christ, we can defeat death, "the unbeatable."

On the flip side, if you don't believe in God and have not recognized Jesus as your Lord and Savior, you are only withstanding the unbeatable. You will die and end up in a place of eternal struggle. Doom and gloom will be upon you for eternity. There is hope, though. Jesus is waiting. Turn to Him!

Are you prepared for curveballs in your game? What preparations could you take? Are you leaning on God even during the good times?

Game Fixing

*For the wages of sin is death, but the gift of
God is eternal life in Christ Jesus our Lord.*

ROMANS 6:23

MOST CASUAL BASEBALL FANS have never heard of "Shoeless" Joe Jackson, but baseball historians know him fairly well. First of all, he gets his nickname of "Shoeless" because he played a game in just his socks because his cleats weren't broken in yet. However, what he is most famous for is the Black Sox Scandal of the 1919 World Series. Joe was one of eight Chicago White Sox players rumored to have been bought off by a bookie to throw the World Series. This is called *game fixing*, in which the results are essentially predetermined so people can win enormous "sure bets." The results of this scandal were immense, and this mistake cost Joe in epic proportions. He was permanently banned from baseball, which included his ability to be inducted into the Hall of Fame (which was basically a shoo-in due to his high level of performance on the field).

In the same way this scandal permanently affected those involved, we can permanently affect our lives by "game fixing." Cheating, lying, pushing the envelope, defying God . . . these are all ways we can "game fix." However, when we do these things, we use the word *sin*. If we allow sin to enter our lives, it can severely deter our chances of defeating the unbeatable.

Game Fixing

Sin is a part of all of our lives. If we are honest with ourselves, we have all sinned. A common thought process is that there are varying levels of sin. In my opinion, "sin is sin." No matter what type of sin we have in our lives, we are to repent of it, and we will be held accountable for our actions when we pass away from this life. In Matthew 12:36, Jesus says that "everyone will have to give account on the day of judgment for every empty word they have spoken." But there is hope, for in Romans 8:1-2, Paul states, "there is now no condemnation for those who are in Christ Jesus, because through Christ Jesus the law of the Spirit who gives life has set you free from the law of sin and death." The key thought is that we are to be in Christ Jesus and not somewhere on the sideline.

There is a problem that comes into play when reading this scripture, though. We are given a choice of whether we want to believe this or not. God has given us free will, and that can have dire consequences. Many people have read the Bible, particularly verses such as Romans 8:1-2, and know what it says by heart. However, just because you know something does not mean you believe it or live it. In order to reap the benefits of the words that Paul says, we must allow the Holy Spirit to change us from the inside out. If we truly believe this and let the Holy Spirit into our lives, it does not mean that we will never sin again. What it does mean is that we will be more cognizant of when we do sin and we will feel led to make better decisions in our daily lives.

Early on in Rachael's battle with cancer, my faith did waver. I had some doubts about how God could let this happen and how He would allow this if He truly loved Rachael. Essentially, I was making it out to be God's fault that Rachael was sick. On the surface, I was walking the walk and talking the talk, but behind closed doors, I struggled with doubt. While I was helping to comfort our family and Rachael, there was a battle brewing inside me, and the devil was gaining some ground. It took a moment of me emotionally exploding in the hospital after Rachael was initially diagnosed for me to realize just how out of touch I was.

By not putting my trust in God and allowing Him to fully take over, I was trusting in myself. As a result, in my opinion, I was sinning against God. He was not pushing me away; I was choosing to push Him away. The amazing thing is that all it took to get to a better place was for me to acknowledge where I was and what I had been doing, and then ask God to be the leader of my life. God is always there; we just need to give Him control.

Are you "game fixing?" Are you pushing God away and trying to take control? What are some things you need to change?

Fans

When Moses' hands grew tired, they took a stone and put it under him and he sat on it. Aaron and Hur held his hands up—one on one side, one on the other—so that his hands remained steady till sunset.

Exodus 17:12

WHEN YOU GO THROUGH something challenging, you want your team in your corner, but having fans is important too. Fans are those who may not always be around you and helping with your every need, but are encouraging and available if necessary. Just like fans for a baseball team, they will not all be relatively close in distance and might even include people you may have never met. This group will look different for each person, but their impact can be huge.

There are varying levels of fans, but their roles are not as specific as the roles for those on your team. While fans do have important roles to help you in your walk, they don't have the same connection (or contract, if you will) that those on your team have. You have those who check in on occasion but are not overly invested, those who root for you consistently and try to watch some games, and those die-hards who would give anything for their team to be successful. Each one of these fans is important to a team. These fans each played a unique role in Rachael's fight. The fans checking in were acquaintances we met through social media or other forms of networking. They are the ones who shared encouraging words and even shared how our story helped them. Those rooting consistently and trying to watch have included neighbors and friends living in other towns. They also shared words of encouragement, but also a hug or other forms of face-to-face support. The die-hards came in many different forms and met different needs, including bringing dinners and taking care of our children.

Having played sports my whole life, I have seen the amazing impact fans can have on a team in a single game or throughout the season. For example, in my junior year of high school, we were not a very good team. However, because we were hosting the state tournament, we were able to participate in it. We got the lowest seed in the tournament and were set to face the best team in the state. They were full of college-level talent, including their starting pitcher, who went on to pitch for Stanford. With the stands loaded with our home team fans, we used their excitement to build a lead prior to the lights literally going out. (I may still have a bit of a sour taste in my mouth over that one.) Unfortunately, the next day when we were able to finish the game, our fans were no longer present, and we ended up losing our momentum and the game. Having our fans in the stands rooting for our success—or not—literally changed the outcome of the game.

Do not be afraid to lean on your fans during this battle. Many of them have been through difficult times in their own lives and can provide inspiration and guidance. Fans will ask what you need or how they can help. Don't be afraid to honestly share with them. This is something I have struggled with, but this struggle has led to additional struggles that wouldn't have arisen if I had simply asked for help. Leaning on your fans could look like simple things, such as asking a neighbor if they could watch your kids for an hour or asking them to go with you for a cup of coffee as an opportunity to step away for a bit. They want to help you, and these are easy ways for them to do so.

How can you better use the fans in your life to help you in your current situation?

Post-Game Celebration

Rejoice always, pray continually, give thanks in all circumstances; for this is God's will for you in Christ Jesus.

1 THESSALONIANS 5:16–18

WHEN A BASEBALL TEAM accomplishes something big, they celebrate. The end of each baseball season is completed with the World Series, which finishes at the end of October or beginning of November. The winning team celebrates with champagne and beer showers in their locker room, which is shrouded in plastic sheets to protect their personal things. This is the highlight that every team yearns for, but there are so many other milestones along the way that teams celebrate. Imagine the following scenarios: your team has beaten your archrival; your team has broken a losing streak; someone on your team reached an individual milestone. These are all things teams celebrate over the course of the year, even though the celebration itself may look different for each success. The same thing should take place when you are facing the unbeatable. Celebrations should not be saved for only big events, like complete healing. While the goal is to have complete healing, there will be opportunities for celebration throughout the season.

When Rachael was diagnosed with a recurrence of her brain cancer in 2016, we initially struggled with trying to celebrate the little things. We were angry with the situation and felt like God's plans were way different than ours. It took us some time to begin seeing and celebrating things that were going well. The diagnosis happened in October, right before the holiday season of Thanksgiving and Christmas. This should have been an easy time to find little things to celebrate, but it was far from a celebratory time. I was also just starting a new job in a new school district, as well as working on my National Board certification and awaiting my previous year's scores. We were under plenty of stress already even before the new diagnosis. Initially, we were consumed by negativity.

God really worked in us during this time and helped us realize that each day is a gift to be celebrated. I know this simple sentence seems easier said than done. Honestly, it was extremely difficult and something we had to be very purposeful in doing. In the Bible, Daniel celebrated many different things in spite of struggles in his life. First, he was taken from his family as a young man to serve in Babylon (Dan 1:3–7). Even through his exile, Daniel continued to praise God and was hopeful and thankful for what he had. Consider when he was thrown into the lions' den to be devoured for his "crimes" (Dan 6:3–16). Upon King Darius's return to the den the next morning, he called out to Daniel to see if he survived and got this response. "Daniel answered, 'May the king live forever! My God sent his angel, and he shut the mouths of the lions. They have not hurt me, because I was found innocent in his sight. Nor have I ever done any wrong before you, Your Majesty" (Dan 6:21–22). Daniel could have been upset that he was thrown into the den, but instead, he took a different approach. As a result of his trust, he stayed upbeat and celebrated. This led to him eventually being very influential in the country and successful in his walk with God.

Using Daniel as inspiration, we moved forward and embraced the little things. One such time was just before Rachael started her new treatments. Our church bought a photography session for us so we could have family pictures. Since part of Rachael's treatment required her head to be shaved, the church made sure we were able to get the pictures while she still had hair. The photoshoot took place over two days and was exhausting as we were fighting our one-year-old, who did not want to sit still, and our four-year-old, who wanted to play with grandma's phone. In spite of the struggles

Post-Game Celebration

and frustrations in the moment, we gained so much from this blessing. Our pictures turned out amazingly, and in looking at them, we were able to celebrate the beauty of the family that God gave us.

The photo shoot was a bigger activity that was easy to celebrate. However, we had many small things that were also worthy of celebrating. These included date nights while friends watched our boys, family Wii bowling nights, and family dinners on the patio. Every day, even when Rachael was not feeling well and didn't want to do anything, still provided opportunities to celebrate. We just had to keep our eyes open and look for them. Keep having those fun times at home and give your loved one the opportunity to watch and enjoy your family's laughter. This simple gift of hearing laughter can help make their day better. I also suggest having a conversation with your loved one about the day's events prior to going to bed each night and sharing some of the good things that happened. This intentionality will help you see the good things as they're happening.

Something that may seem odd for those dealing with treatments of any kind is having celebrations on treatment days, but maybe there is a small treat that can become part of those days to make them something to look forward to. For us, it involved going through the coffee shop and getting a special coffee that we normally would not get. Maybe for you, it is ice cream or even a favorite type of candy. Another option could be doing something for others going through these difficulties, such as bringing little gifts of love to others to help give them a little boost. There are countless ideas. Give it a try.

Where are some areas you could be celebrating? Are you only focusing on big things and missing little things?

Off-Season

Therefore put on the full armor of God, so that when the day of evil comes, you may be able to stand your ground, and after you have done everything, to stand.

EPHESIANS 6:13

ONE KEY PIECE IN the life of a baseball player is the off-season. The word *off* can be confusing to those not involved in sports. Many people believe this is when players simply unwind and take it easy. This may include family vacations or going to a second home and getting away from it all. That is partially true. However, the off-season is primarily for healing up and preparing for the upcoming season. This is where the player will begin working out to get their body in better shape. The types of workouts players do in the off-season are much more strenuous due to not having to play games.

If you are working on truly defeating the unbeatable, you will come into off-season times. Some of these may only last a couple of months and some may last many years. For me and Rachael, it was over five years. During this time, we did a lot of recovery (in regards to Rachael's health) and began conditioning in a slightly different way. We finished our college degrees, I received a teaching job, and we traveled to Turkey and Greece. We also became more involved in our church and built different relationships with God and with each other. These relationships turned out to be key when the "games" returned.

OFF-SEASON

It is very easy to take time to just relax and not worry about anything. This is fine for a short while. I don't mean that you can't enjoy life and be happy. What I mean is that if you are fighting cancer or a disease, it is possible it will return. Please understand that evil is lying in wait to find areas and times of vulnerability and will pounce. This happened to us with Rachael's recurrence. Before it happened, we celebrated the births of our two boys, who Rachael was never supposed to have been able to have. We bought our own house and built a strong family. However, we slowly began letting our guard down with regard to the possibility of her cancer returning. Part of this was due to the way her doctors acted toward her and part was due to the way Rachael was feeling and doing. With all of the success she was having, the doctors began calling her the "poster patient," so to speak. The idea of recurrence was far from our minds because they were calling her stable. That is why, when we got the news that Rachael's cancer was back, we felt like we had just been sucker-punched.

Something I want to note here is that the concept of "stable" or "cancer-free" is something to be excited about and should be celebrated. However, please remember that cancer cells are so small that they can't always be picked up with scans, so it is still very possible that you could still have some in your body. (This information came directly from our doctors, so you know it came from a medical professional, not just me.) This was something we struggled with and didn't understand.

The Israelites went through their own version of the off-season after they had been freed from slavery. God provided for them daily with food and water (Exod 16:4–5). Several times, He gave them direction through Moses of how to live, and for many years they were successful. However, their ranks were slowly infiltrated by evil ideas and false gods. As a result, they were caught off guard about what was happening, and this caused them to fall into times of great struggle. By continuing to praise and follow God's commands, they could have prevented these various struggles.

Now, getting news like "your cancer is back" is never easy. However, if we had continued to prepare and "work out" during our off-season, our response to this news would have been different. I am not saying that we would have walked around with smiles on our faces and acted excited about the news. When trials come, frustration and grief are a part of the process. The difference is in how you think through the news. If you have been preparing during the off-season, you will still have emotions of grief and frustration. But you will search for God's presence and trust in His plan, and you will treasure small blessings and time with your loved ones. Time is something we can't ever get back, so please take every moment treasuring the time you are given with your loved ones.

Another aspect of the off-season is a chance to look back over the previous season and decide how you can change. For baseball players, that involves looking at film and talking with their coaches and fellow players about what they notice. To one player, it may seem that they are dropping their elbow, which is causing them to hit the lower half of the baseball and hit a lot of pop-ups, while to another player it may seem like the problem is a weak lower half. Being able to use this time to work on making corrections and plan for the upcoming season is very important.

Doing this planning can carry you a long way in future seasons. This is definitely something we did not do with our team. Rachael and I had conversations with each other, but were not intentional in asking others what they noticed about us and how we could be better prepared. Intentionality is the key to success in this situation. The number one suggestion I would have to help you prepare during the off-season is to be in the Word. The Bible provides any support and guidance you will ever need to be successful. Another suggestion I have for this time is to find support groups for your type of illness and become involved. If you have lots of good things happening, you can be a support for those going through the season of fighting. Also, sharing stories with those who have been in the off-season and are now going through a new season will help you in your own preparations if you do encounter a new season.

Are you currently in an off-season? If so, how can you use this time more effectively?

Love of Game

May the God of hope fill you with all joy and peace as you trust in him, so that you may overflow with hope by the power of the Holy Spirit.

ROMANS 15:13

GENERALLY SPEAKING, THERE ARE two types of baseball players. The first type of player loves the game and just so happens to make good money. This player shows up each day ready to put in the work, understanding there will be ups and downs but believing it will be worth it in the end. To them, a bad day at the baseball field is better than a good day just about anywhere else. The second type of player is in it for the money. These are the players who are always looking for the next big payday. These players are just as good as the first type and work just as hard. However, the joy they gain from the actual playing of the game is much different than those who play for the love of the game they grew up playing.

In the same way, we have a choice every day of how we are going to react to the things that happen to us, whether things are going well for us or we are going through trying times. Life is full of ups and downs, and our attitude directly affects the way we live. Our love of life and our attitudes toward it are largely impacted by the way we are brought up. If we come from a loving and positive family with a good outlook on life, we may be more willing to keep an upbeat attitude during trying times. However, if we come from a family that struggled and was always negative and down, it can be more difficult to have a positive outlook. It doesn't mean you can't have a positive outlook at all—it may just require a bit more work on your part to make that happen.

To truly have a love for life, one piece that we really need is God. Having Him on our side gives us hope and perspective that those who do not know Him will never understand. When we are going through trying times, He is going through them with us. When we are going through great times, He is with us. He never leaves us, no matter how distant He feels. Romans 5 is a great reminder of this. Verses 1 and 2 state: "Therefore, since we have been justified through faith, we have peace with God through our Lord Jesus Christ, through whom we have gained access by faith into this grace in which we now stand. And we boast in the hope of the glory of God." Even through the most difficult moments, we can be sure that God will give peace to those who trust in Him.

In our own walk, there were times when God felt distant or not even present at all. Seeing Rachael after her surgery when she couldn't respond and being told her cancer was back both left me at a loss. Each time, I questioned whether God was really with us. However, each time, someone from our team helped me realize that God was still with us. In those moments, I was the player "doing it for the money." On game day, I was showing up and performing, but when it wasn't game time, I was totally unfocused. If I had been like the player who does it for the love of the game, these hard moments would have been better and my attitude would have been much different. Just like when a hitter needs to keep his weight back just a little bit longer so he can hit effectively, a slight attitude adjustment can be helpful in moments of difficulty.

Romans 15:5-6 is extremely helpful to consider when it comes to attitude. It states: "May the God who gives endurance and encouragement give you the same attitude of mind toward each other that Christ Jesus had, so that with one mind and one voice you may glorify the God and Father of our Lord Jesus Christ." By having a more positive attitude in hard situations, I could have seen the encouragement God was giving me from our team. I would have seen that He was already giving me the endurance in this fight. I would have seen the opportunity to glorify God in the moment.

What type of player are you right now? What could you change to help you and those on your team?

Closer

The end of a matter is better than its beginning, and patience is better than pride.

ECCLESIASTES 7:8

WITH THE MANY TWEAKS to rules and regulations over the years and advances in technology, the game of baseball has changed in many ways. One of the biggest changes is how managers now use their pitchers. In the early to mid-1900s, starting pitchers typically pitched most, if not all, of the innings of each game they played. However, now most starting pitchers now go five or six innings and that is about it. As a result, the job of closer has become a key role. Their number one job when they go into a game is to get the final three outs of the game. The expectation is that they come into the game and slam the door shut on the chances for the other team to come back and win.

Many of the current closers in major league baseball are considered "flamethrowers." In other words, they throw HARD. The average fastball thrown by major league pitchers has been around 93 miles per hour for the past few years, which is up from what it used to be, but compared to many closers, that is slow. The closers of this time period typically throw 98 to 100 miles per hour, and in fact, several have been "gunned" throwing several miles per hour over 100. So when I say they come in to slam the door shut on the other team, they do it with authority.

CLOSER

In the same way that closers finish with authority, defeating the unbeatable also requires authority in how you finish. Your authority can be grounded in the fact that God is with you and has His hands in everything, that you feel comfortable in the knowledge that you enjoyed the time God blessed you with, and that through all the curveballs Satan threw at you, you made adjustments and successfully defeated him.

I know that each person reading this is at a different part in their journey. Some of you are struggling with the thought of your loved one passing away (or passing away yourself). Others of you have already experienced this loss and are looking for encouragement. As I write this chapter, I am walking through this part of Rachael's journey. God blessed us with over ten amazing years of marriage and two beautiful boys we were never supposed to have, so I get the struggle. I know that it is hard and that there is no how-to book to get you through this. I am certainly no expert. However, through God and His Word, there is a pathway to life after the death of a loved one.

I firmly believe that God gave us each of our loved ones for a reason. Maybe it was to help you in your walk, maybe it was for you to help them, or maybe it was for you to work with them to help someone else. The greatest part about defeating the unbeatable is knowing where your loved one is. They aren't spending eternity in the burning sulfur and misery of hell. They are in heaven with our Father. They are no longer in pain or suffering. They are free. Life in this world is just a blink of an eye in the grand scheme of things. If we stay on the correct path and follow Jesus, someday we'll be reunited with our loved ones.

Closing is not an easy job, and it is not for the faint of heart ... at least, not if you want to be good at it. With God, though, we can take comfort in knowing that even when our worlds feel like they are falling apart, He truly does have a plan. We live in the here and now, and during our time on earth that is our complete focus. However, God works on a much different time scale. He knows the plans He has for us, and they are so much bigger than we can possibly imagine.

DEFEATING THE UNBEATABLE

My favorite Bible verse speaks specifically about this. Jeremiah 29:11 says, "'For I know the plans I have for you,' declares the Lord, 'plans to prosper you and not to harm you, plans to give you hope and a future.'" I think this verse gets interpreted incorrectly quite frequently. I think it is typically read more as "plans to prosper you *with wealth and comfort* and not to harm you *with diseases and struggles*, plans to give you hope and a future *on earth*" (emphasis mine). Honestly, if we follow God, our hope and our future are with Him. We will see our lives from His perspective when we stand with Him and see the new heaven and new earth.

God has never left you or your loved one. When we feel that He is not close, it is because of us, not Him. He is always there, waiting expectantly for us to turn, and as soon as He sees that slight turn, He fully embraces us. So if you feel like God is distant, whether you are going through darkness or light, check the dipstick in your relationship with Him. I know several times I have done this and realized I was preventing Him from speaking to me. I know that simply getting back into the rhythms of my daily life will bring me closer to God and help me refocus, and at that point, I am able to feel God's presence.

So even though closing out one's life is not an easy thing, it can be done with authority. Embrace God's love for you and your loved one in spite of the tragedy, because He does. Understand that His heart is breaking just as much as yours is, if not more. He does not want His children to suffer, but with this broken world, suffering happens.

Think about how amazing it will be when you are alive in heaven and look back and realize all the things that might have never been if you had chosen not to close with authority—if you had chosen the easy route and blamed God or even decided that He didn't exist. Both of these are real things that happen, but where are they going to get you? You are within one out of winning the World Series and being the hero as the closer, and now you decide it's too hard and bail on your team. Next thing you know, the game is over and everyone you worked so hard with has left because they put their trust in God, but you didn't.

Second Timothy 4:7 states, "I have fought the good fight, I have finished the race, I have kept the faith." Each part of this verse is important, but we must also understand the apostle Paul's context. In this passage, he was writing to Timothy about a time when people will turn away from God. They will focus on the things they want to hear through false teachings. Now you may say, "but this was written about 1,900 years ago and doesn't apply to us." To that I say, look around this world and ask yourself, "are things different?" We have people who spend their entire lives trying to make others think highly of them and people who "brainwash" others into following their way of thinking. Things are the same as when Paul wrote this letter; the players are just different. Those who stand firm in their belief in God's goodness without wavering are the ones who will have fought the good fight, finished the race, and kept the faith.

Take a look around you right now. How many different devices do you have within reach? As I write this, I have three devices within reach. On each one, I can access social media and other parts of the internet within seconds and conduct a quick search to find instances of people trying to dissuade other people from believing in God. I can also find instances of people acting like the Pharisees and condemning anyone who is not living the way they think is right. This is not how we will bring people to the Lord. Close strong by being a loving and compassionate person who trusts God. That is how others will come to Jesus. If you are not a Christ follower or have walked away from the faith due to others condemning you, know that Jesus is waiting for you and loves you.

Are you finishing strong? What areas do you need to slam the door shut on?

Retirement

*I have fought the good fight, I have finished
the race, I have kept the faith.*

2 TIMOTHY 4:7

WHEN A BASEBALL PLAYER has played all the games their body can take or feels it is time to move forward with other opportunities, they retire. Most of the time this happens in their thirties, though some are older and some younger. Some players are lucky to leave healthy, while others leave due to injury. Many players will look back at their careers and reflect on their accomplishments. Did they win All-Star accolades, batting titles, Cy Young Awards, Gold Glove Awards, MVP honors, World Series rings, series pennants, and so on?

If a player has made a big enough impact during their career, they can be voted by a panel into the Major League Baseball Hall of Fame in Cooperstown, New York. At the time of publication, there have been 268 players voted into the Hall of Fame. If they have made a major impact within their organization, they can look forward to possibly having their jersey number retired. This means that no other person within that organization will wear that number again. These are all high honors that baseball-playing kids grow up dreaming of achieving for themselves. I personally grew up pretending to be some of my favorite players, such as Tom Glavine pitching in Game Seven of the World Series, leading my team to victory.

Retirement

While these accolades are great, realistically, they are just a statue of a head that looks somewhat like the player and a plaque with their name on it. Yes, when people say their names, fans remember them and maybe some of their stats or even specific things they did in a certain game, but will they know about the person? More often than not, no.

In baseball, when you are finished in your career, you are done playing. However, if you defeat the unbeatable and finish running your race and end up passing away, that is not the end. God has promised us in His word that all things will be made new. In Revelation 21:4 it states, "He will wipe every tear from their eyes. There will be no more death or mourning or crying or pain, for the old order of things has passed away." If you have chosen to defeat the unbeatable instead of trying to withstand it, your life does not end when the inevitable ends. On the contrary, it is just beginning. We will all pass away, but it's your choice where you will end up.

When Jesus died on the cross, He took all of our sins upon Himself to save us. This freedom from sin is offered to us with one caveat: we must welcome Jesus into our hearts and allow Him to change us. There are two key parts to that last sentence. First, welcoming someone is a verb, which means that it requires an action of some kind. Specifically, in this situation, we must confess that Jesus is our Lord and Savior. The second key part of that sentence is that we must want Him to have complete authority in our life. It is an acknowledgment that we need Him and we cannot be our best selves without Him. Without that commitment on our part, when we get to the day of judgment, we will hear the unfortunate words, "Depart from me, you who are cursed, into the eternal fire prepared for the devil and his angels" (Matt 25:41).

The following is a poem I wrote in high school that I feel captures this concept in a very specific way.

"FINAL WALK"

In my dream I was an old man
Walking down a divine road

Looking back at my life and what I had accomplished
Then passed on to a greater life.

Because of my faith in God and my acknowledgement of Him as my Lord and Savior, this dream can become my reality. That divine road I am walking down is leading me to the gate of heaven, where my life will be just beginning. It will not be a sentence of permanent agony.

So often we get caught up in the here and now and forget that this life is just a moment in time. Jesus died on the cross for our eternity. Death is not the end for those who believe, but just the beginning. So instead of trying to worry about everything, take time to enjoy your life and worry about the one important thing you *can* control by giving your life to God. Each day is a precious gift that we are to not take for granted.

As a spouse or caretaker, the idea of retirement takes on a different meaning. We are left to try and prepare for continuing on in our lives without our loved ones. This is a very difficult thing to do. Remember these words from Joshua 1:9: "Have I not commanded you? Be strong and courageous. Do not be afraid; do not be discouraged, for the Lord your God will be with you wherever you go." God is with you and holding you; lean on him.

Have you given your life to God? If not what is preventing you from doing it? Are you ready for "retirement?"

All chapters up to this point were written prior to Rachael's passing. The following chapters were written after she passed.

Grieving in the Victory

For our light and momentary troubles are achieving for us an eternal glory that far outweighs them all.

2 CORINTHIANS 4:17

AS A PITCHER IN baseball, you are basically the one controlling the game. You choose when to throw a pitch, pick off to a base, or step off the rubber. You are in control. However, some external sources can throw a wrench in that control and cause grief for a time.

When I was thirteen years old, my All-Star team was playing in our state tournament and I was pitching. There were runners on first base and third base, we were leading, and it was the last inning. Looking back, I am not sure why I decided to pick off to first base, but I did. I did my normal move and picked to first. This is something I did a lot, and I had a pretty good move. I did everything the same as I always did, but for some reason, I did not throw the ball. On some pickoff moves, this is not a big deal. For me, this was a huge deal, since I was a left-handed pitcher and by using the move I was required to throw to the base. As a result, there was a balk called on me, and each runner got to move up a base, tying the baseball game and rattling me enough to lose the game.

As an athlete, this caused me a lot of grief, and I held on to that mistake for a long time. On the other hand, though, it did push me to grow and get better so that situation didn't happen again.

Defeating the Unbeatable

Two years later, I was able to get my redemption; not only was I in a similar situation in a state championship game but I came out as the winning pitcher. I used my grief as motivation to learn and better myself.

In the Bible, David is a key example of someone who starts out with adversity. He had been anointed and chosen by God to be king of Israel, but he had to go into hiding from King Saul when Saul became jealous of him (1 Sam 19:1–2). Finally, after many years, he was finally able to take his place as king. He used those years of being on the run as motivation, and with God by his side, he became a great king.

Up to this point I have talked about areas involving both the person fighting illness (cancer in our case) and the supporter or caregiver. This chapter is written from a different perspective. On Christmas morning of 2017, my beautiful wife Rachael was taken home to be with her heavenly Father. So instead of explaining how to live for both, this chapter is geared toward those who must continue on alone.

You see, defeating the unbeatable does not simply end when our loved one passes. The devil is now going to move from pitching his best five pitchers to his top one or two. He knows that you are vulnerable and questioning so many things. He is using his best ammunition to find a way to break through your defenses. Ephesians 6:11 states, "Put on the full armor of God, so that you can take your stand against the devil's schemes." The devil is not a one-trick pony; he uses so many different things, including using partial biblical truths, to get you. God will help you withstand these attacks if you put your trust in Him and put His full armor on.

On several occasions, the devil has tried nudging the door of my heart open just enough to see if I will stop him or if I will fail to notice him and allow him to open it a bit more. Failing to notice him is very easy in times like these. The numbness, the lack of motivation, and the exhaustion make it easy to ignore what is going on around us. These feelings are all normal and it is okay to have them, but we must keep our guard up against the devil. Having a good group of teammates around you will be extremely helpful in combatting these advances. Throughout our loved ones' battles, we were also in battle. Now we are being attacked in our most vulnerable state.

It is like when a starting pitcher has given all he has and the manager comes out and asks the pitcher if he has anything left in the tank for just one more inning. The competitive side of a player will want to say that they do have more and want to continue. However, that answer means the pitcher is relying on his own strength. Instead, saying "I have given everything, so bring in somebody fresh" is an important step. Understanding our weaknesses allows for greater opportunity for growth and closeness with God. Grieving magnifies those weaknesses.

Jesus was put through a test of His strength when He was in the wilderness for forty days. In Matthew 4:1-2 it says, "Jesus was led by the Spirit into the wilderness to be tempted by the devil. After fasting forty days and forty nights, he was hungry." Think about this for a moment: Jesus was fully human, so not eating for forty days would have been extremely difficult and painful. A quick Google search shows that, on average, a person can last about three weeks without food. Jesus went almost six! Through this lens, we can suspect that anyone's defenses would be weakened. However, with each temptation, Jesus put His trust in God and stood up to the devil. Finally, the devil left Jesus alone, and Jesus relied on angels sent by God to minister to Him to help Him heal.

There are many facets to the grieving process and lots of books out there to help with each step. However, one major point I have learned since Rachael's passing is that everybody grieves differently and at different speeds. Just because one person cries every day and can't seem to function while another person gets back to work quickly doesn't mean either one is doing it better or worse. I took a month off of work to be with my boys. Upon returning to work, I definitely had some difficult days, and I noticed people giving each other looks and whispering to each other if I was doing all right. However, for me, getting back to work and some normalcy was very important and helpful in my grieving process. This is the time where your team needs to be your go-to. You'll need people you can confide in and share your struggles with. Being vulnerable and sharing your weaknesses with trusted friends and mentors actually shows amazing strength. Remember Jesus being tempted by Satan (Matt 4:1–11)? At the end of this time, Jesus was beat down and struggling, but He didn't try to regroup on His own, even though He could have. He allowed angels to come to Him and help Him get better.

Through my grieving process, I learned a lot about my ability to lean on others. I was always the rock, as I talked about earlier, so it was hard for me to open up. Luckily, I had a small core group of men who I met regularly for breakfast. This small group of God-loving men helped me work through difficult situations and allowed me to be completely open. This was a very uncomfortable thing for me in the beginning, but I knew I needed something. Taking the initiative to ask other people if they were interested in being in this group was scary. However, the benefits were beyond what I could have imagined. The men I asked felt like they needed something like this too, but felt similar to me when it came to being proactive about asking. Not only was I blessed through this group but the other men were as well. In my mind, I felt I could have pushed through and continued to be everyone's rock, but God placed these men in my life for a specific reason, and I am incredibly thankful for them.

Be prepared to open up to people when you are ready. People truly do want to be there for you, but if you aren't willing to be vulnerable, they won't know what to do. In the beginning, it is hard to even get dressed and eat anything, and you truly don't even know what you need. Your world seems to have fallen apart, and it's okay to have those feelings. However, if you take one piece of advice from this whole book, let it be this: don't be afraid to ask for the silliest-seeming things when people ask you if they can help. If you are at home and someone is there with you and asks how they can help and the garbage needs to be taken out, ask them to do that. If you have a young child and they need a diaper change, ask for someone to do that.

I know these things sound trivial, but it allows others to help you in practical ways, and this practice will help you get used to asking for help so when you truly have bigger needs, you will be more willing to ask. Romans 12:5 says that "in Christ we, though many, form one body, and each member belongs to all the others."

Christ has put people around you to help you. Lean on them. Having conversations with these people who were willing to help me but weren't sure how really opened my eyes. Let's be honest—everyone knows you are going through a hard time, but if you put on a strong face and tell everyone that you are doing fine, it's difficult for those who are willing to help. This will eventually lead them to stop asking. Then you will reach a breaking point and wonder where everyone went. It may feel like you went from having so many people around that you could hardly breathe to wondering if you stink so bad that nobody wants to be around you. They haven't gone anywhere; they are still there. You just need to be vulnerable.

Can you identify those who are trying to help you? Is there a small, close group of people with beliefs similar to yours who you feel comfortable sharing your struggles with? In which areas do you need support?

Confidence

"With him is only the arm of flesh, but with us is the Lord our God to help us and to fight our battles." And the people gained confidence from what Hezekiah the king of Judah said.

2 CHRONICLES 32:8

WHEN IT COMES TO successful professional baseball players and coaches, there is one quality that all of them have: confidence. They have talent, but they also have confidence in their ability to hit a baseball, catch a baseball, or accurately throw a pitch. If a player doesn't have confidence in these areas, they won't be successful and will lose their position. Coaches, in the same way, must have confidence in the decisions they make. If they second-guess each of their decisions, then their players will lose confidence in them and the team's productivity will suffer.

However, confidence has an evil cousin that can cause problems: arrogance. When a player is arrogant, it means they may be extremely gifted, but they believe that they can't do anything wrong. They are the players who are often referred to as toxic teammates. They exude negativity that is detrimental to their teams. Typically, these players are quite successful on an individual level, but when adversity comes, they often struggle.

When you are going through struggles with an illness, grief, or moving forward in your life after a hard time, it is important to have

Confidence

confidence. However, just like with baseball players, it is important to take care to not become arrogant. Isaiah 13:11 states, "I will punish the world for its evil, the wicked for their sins. I will put an end to the arrogance of the haughty and will humble the pride of the ruthless." Isaiah is making some extremely important points. First, we live in a world full of evil. At every corner, there is evil waiting to try and derail your life. This evil may be illness, people, or negative situations. Second, he states that arrogance is wicked and a sin. Therefore, it is key for us to focus on preventing arrogance from entering our hearts.

There is one foolproof way to prevent arrogance and gain confidence: by being in the Word. The Bible is full of game plans and training opportunities to help you become more confident. Deuteronomy 31:6 tells us, "Be strong and courageous. Do not be afraid or terrified . . . for the Lord your God goes with you; he will never leave you nor forsake you." This is another verse that tells us where to focus our thoughts. The only way we can truly be strong and have confidence in everything is through the Lord. By putting your confidence in the Lord, He will always go with you, even in the darkest times.

In high school, I was confident in my abilities as a pitcher. I had the ability to throw pitches where I wanted to and make the ball move in different directions. With all of these things working in my favor, my confidence would occasionally turn into arrogance. I would stand on the mound feeling like I was unstoppable. I would make excuses when things didn't work out the way I wanted them to. This arrogance eventually caught up with me and prevented me from reaching my full potential. My freshman year in college, I suddenly lost my confidence in being able to throw a baseball to bases, which is a big part of being a pitcher. While I was still able to pitch, I wasn't able to field my position. As a result, opposing teams felt confident in bunting the ball toward me and could take larger leads on the bases since they knew I wasn't able to throw to the bases.

Dealing with this shortcoming took a lot out of me. I spent extra time at the field working on my own, practicing throwing to bases. I listened to podcasts of experts who help athletes with barriers like mine. However, once I was back in a game and an opposing player got on a base or I had to throw to a base, my anxiety went through the roof. I had lost my focus, my confidence.

In the same way, we can easily be distracted by our struggles. When things are at their darkest and you feel lost, confidence easily disappears, and it is difficult to get back. We begin looking for help anywhere we can. We look for a quick fix that will make us feel good and make everything better. More often than not, we find things that may help in the short term, but do not actually build our confidence back up for the long term. The only way to truly do this is through Jesus. Get your confidence back and move forward by trusting in Him.

Where is your confidence level? Are there areas of your life where you are overconfident to the point of arrogance? What have been some negative effects of arrogance in your life? How will you prevent these things from happening again?

Second Career

Yet this I call to mind and therefore I have hope: Because of the Lord's great love we are not consumed, for his compassions never fail. They are new every morning; great is your faithfulness.

LAMENTATIONS 3:21–23

SINCE MOST BASEBALL PLAYERS retire at relatively young ages compared to other occupations, they often find second careers. It may be working a new job for the team they previously played for, such as a coach or an advisor to the coaches, or they may get a job in the team's front office helping to make the team better. Many will find careers outside of baseball in completely different fields, like business or education. For those going through loss, this second career may look like moving to a new area and starting fresh, finding a new hobby, or find a new love.

As I stated earlier, each person grieves differently. I am not trying to push anyone into things they are not comfortable with. However, remember that for others, this may be what they are ready for. Moving out of the home where you and your loved one lived may be challenging for you and something you definitely don't want to do. If this is how it is for you, don't allow others to push you into selling because they believe it is right for you. If you feel like selling your house will help you in your grieving process, then do what is best for you.

Defeating the Unbeatable

After my Grandpa Ed's passing, my Grandma Joy kept the house they'd lived in together for many years. There were times when she didn't spend much time there and "lived" with my family about an hour and a half away for a few years, but she wanted to hold on to the house, and she did so until she was ready to part with it. On the flip side, I put the house Rachael and I bought together and lived in for more than three years up for sale just over a year after she passed. To others, this may seem too fast, but for me it was right. Just remember that you are the one making the decisions; however, you are never alone and always have an ear available to you. God is ready to have you lean on Him, and all you have to do is talk to Him. In 1 Kings 9:3 it states: "The Lord said to him: 'I have heard the prayer and plea you have made before me; I have consecrated this temple, which you have built, by putting my Name there forever. My eyes and my heart will always be there.'" Nobody knows your heart and what is best for you more than our heavenly Father. Go to Him and share your feelings, worries, and hopes. He is ready to listen!

I know that this may be a very controversial thought process, and many people will say that the experts recommend one thing or another, but please remember this is just one person's view on this situation. I am not saying ignore those who support you, because they are trying to look out for you. What I am saying is that they are probably grieving as well and may be at a different place in their grief. Be willing to acknowledge their thoughts, but don't let them bully you into something you feel strongly about. Understand that you need to do you. You can try something and realize that you actually aren't ready and take a step back. You can take up a hobby you have always wanted to try; it may be a bust, but it may help you and be a source of motivation. You can go on a date and feel great, or you can feel uncomfortable and know that you are not ready yet and put dating on the back burner. There is no one-size-fits-all solution when it comes to grief!

Jesus received counsel from His disciples about going to Jerusalem, where they knew things would not go well. Peter always ready to share his true thinking specifically tells Jesus "Never Lord. . . . .This shall never happen to you!" (Matthew 16:22). Jesus

Second Career

had told them about His upcoming suffering, death, and resurrection as a sign to all. Jesus heard his disciples' concerns, but also knew what needed to be done because He was in constant counsel with God. Jesus knew what was expected of Him because He spent time in prayer about this specific situation. In fact, in the garden of Gethsemane, we are told Jesus went away by Himself to pray to God three separate times up until the very moment He was handed over to be beaten and killed. If Jesus, the Son of God, who was all-knowing and in constant communication with God, prayed like this in times of struggle, what is preventing you from doing this as well? Jesus, in His human nature, was fighting a battle between His own will and God's will, but the most important thing to consider is that He finished each prayer with "yet not my will, but yours be done" (Luke 22:42). Jesus knew to put complete trust in His Father and that, in the end, everything would be used for His glory.

Jesus's twelve disciples, who had lived with Him for three years and witnessed many of His miracles and teachings, had their own opinions. At times during their travels, they gave Jesus advice out of what they felt was love. But as Jesus stated in Matthew 16:23 in response to Peter, "Get behind me, Satan! You are a stumbling block to me; you do not have in mind the concerns of God, but merely human concerns." Jesus knew things that the disciples did not and could not understand. They just knew from their human perspective what their feelings were about the situation.

What is even more amazing is that this worldly advice came from Peter, who ended up being one of the most influential figures in early Christianity. He wrote two books of the Bible and was the first leader of the Christian church. In Matthew 16:16, Peter responded to Jesus's question about who they thought he was by saying, "You are the Messiah, the Son of the living God." Peter knew exactly who Jesus was and what had been foretold about Him, but he still fought it.

In the same way, there may be times when people try to talk you out of doing something because of their own feelings. You will have ups and downs as you walk through this phase of your journey. Even when you feel that you are doing what is best for you, you will still have struggles. Just keep your head up and keep looking forward to whatever your goal is for your life.

For me, I was lucky enough to meet an amazing woman, Tasha, about seven months after Rachael's passing. I spent a lot of time praying about this situation and felt completely affirmed by God that she was the woman I was meant to be with. At each stage in our relationship, people expressed concerns or thoughts about us. I heard things like "Are you sure you are ready?" or "You should slow down." While these people were trying to be helpful with their advice, they were all still going through their own grief processes, and their own feelings clouded their judgment of my grief process.

Tasha and I spent a lot of time early on in our relationship talking about what I had been through. For the first month of our relationship, we didn't even meet face-to-face. We spent that entire time getting to know each other and have open, honest communication about our faith and hopes for our lives. In these conversations, we openly acknowledged and discussed how some people would try to find ways to deter us from continuing our relationship.

As we continued through the early stages of our relationship, that is exactly what happened. People made subtle (or not-so-subtle) comments, some of which may have been intentional and some of which may have been ignorant of how we received them. There were many evenings Tasha and I spent just holding each other as our emotions spilled over because of what was happening. We both firmly believed that God put us together, as we had both prayed a lot for what we wanted and felt that we were the answers to each other's prayers, so why were we being treated like this?

Once we got engaged, it felt like the devil began pushing harder in his attempts to separate us through distractions. In Romans 12:2, we are warned of this: "Do not conform to the pattern of this world, but be transformed by the renewing of your mind. Then you will be able to test and approve what God's will is—his good, pleasing and perfect will." The world tried to make us conform to their thinking and fought what we felt was God's will for us. Luckily, we still had our core group of fellow believers who we trusted. They helped keep us focused and moving forward toward our wedding day. Not only did they support us by providing comfort but they also went to bat for us in conversations with naysayers.

There were several times when Tasha and I just wanted to elope and be married as a way to end the hurtful and frustrating comments about our relationship. This seemed like it would have sped up the process to us, but to others, our entire relationship had seemed to move at a quick pace. We started dating at the end of July 2018, got engaged that Thanksgiving, and got married the following June. In fact, Tasha's sister joked about the length of our relationship during her toast at our wedding. While to others this relationship has been quick, through prayers and trust in God, Tasha and I both know without a shadow of a doubt that this marriage has God's blessing. Song of Songs 8:6–7 states this perfectly:

> Place me like a seal over your heart,
>   like a seal on your arm;
> for love is as strong as death,
>   its jealousy unyielding as the grave.
> It burns like blazing fire,
>   like a mighty flame.
> Many waters cannot quench love;
>   rivers cannot sweep it away.
> If one were to give
>   all the wealth of one's house for love,
>   it would be utterly scorned.

We did not let the waters and rivers wash away our love, but rather we used them as motivation to strengthen our relationship.

I experienced changes "quickly" after Rachael's passing, according to "the experts" and people close to me. However, I felt and continue to feel really good about the changes I made, not only for me but for our sons and for Tasha. We are building a life together and moving forward exactly the way Rachael wanted; she shared her wishes with me as we walked through her journey together. Right now, you may be thinking, "Craig, you are completely crazy!" Maybe my situation is very unique, but it was the smartest decision for me and my family. Your situation may be completely different, and that's okay; just trust in God and let him guide you through the process.

I want to remind you of something super important, spelled out in Proverbs 27:1: "Do not boast about tomorrow, for you do not know what a day may bring." We are not guaranteed tomorrow; we aren't guaranteed anything. Life is very precious, and if you are reading this book, you have experienced firsthand just how true this statement is. Be willing to do something for yourself, through faith and understanding. Love your family, love God, and defeat the unbeatable.

Are there decisions in your life that you are currently fighting? Have you prayed about them? Why aren't you making those changes?